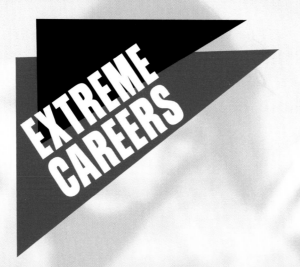

EXTREME CAREERS

BODYGUARDS

Life Protecting Others

John Giacobello

the rosen publishing group's
rosen
central

Published in 2003 by The Rosen Publishing Group, Inc.
29 East 21st Street, New York, NY 10010

First Edition 2003

Library of Congress Cataloging-in-Publication Data

Giacobello, John
Bodyguards : life protecting others / John Giacobello.
    p. cm. — (Extreme careers)
Includes bibliographical references and index.
Summary: This book describes the careers of bodyguards, individuals who must be security engineers and planners, responsible for all aspects of their clients' safety.
ISBN 0-8239-3795-X (lib.)
1. Bodyguards   2. Celebrities—Protection
3. Private security services—Vocational guidance
HV8290.G53 2002
363.28'9—dc21

                          2002-012246

Manufactured in the United States of America

Contents

Introduction

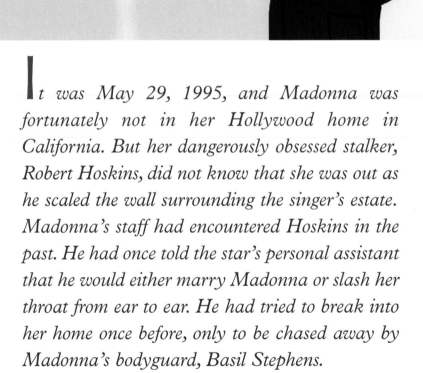

It was May 29, 1995, and Madonna was fortunately not in her Hollywood home in California. But her dangerously obsessed stalker, Robert Hoskins, did not know that she was out as he scaled the wall surrounding the singer's estate. Madonna's staff had encountered Hoskins in the past. He had once told the star's personal assistant that he would either marry Madonna or slash her throat from ear to ear. He had tried to break into her home once before, only to be chased away by Madonna's bodyguard, Basil Stephens.

Now Stephens was face-to-face with his client's mad follower once more. Before entering the estate, Hoskins had announced into the intercom that he *was Madonna's husband and that he intended to kill everybody in the house. The high-profile bodyguard needed to act quickly.*

Stephens confronted the intruder, who lunged at him. Believing that Hoskins was trying to strangle him, he fired his gun at him twice, not knowing where the bullets would hit or if Hoskins would die. It was the first time in his career Stephens had ever shot another person.

The shaken bodyguard told the bleeding man, "There's an ambulance on the way. I'm sorry I shot you." Hoskins replied, "No problem."

Sound like an average workday? It is not really average for anyone, but bodyguards never know what wild experiences might await them when they begin an assignment. Personal protection is a career filled with danger, action, and surprise. So what does it take to be a bodyguard? Do they just follow celebrities around and look scary, like the hulks we see on television? Is there more to it than pulverizing reporters and taking bullets for the president?

Today's bodyguards are more than just tall escorts. They are security engineers and planners, responsible

Bodyguards, such as this one escorting Madonna from her vehicle, protect their clients from threats and danger on a daily basis.

for all aspects of their clients' safety. That takes brains as well as muscle, not to mention an ability to work under intense pressure and build strong relationships. But perhaps it is bodyguards' loyalty and courage in the face of danger to themselves, most of all, that draws them into a life of protecting others. This book is about these courageous souls and their work, and a career that can be described only as extreme.

Dangerous World

1

Reading the news can be shocking. Violence seems to be everywhere, and scary things can happen right around the corner. It's enough to make you wonder what kind of a world we live in.

Is it a dangerous world? It can be. We are all at risk, and we do the best we can to protect ourselves. We keep strong locks on our doors, avoid walking alone at night, and sometimes even take classes to learn self-defense. But we also know that we can go about our daily lives with a reasonably low risk of violence. We can go to the park, take the subway, walk the dog, or buy groceries. Chances are pretty good that we will not be harmed as long as we keep our eyes and ears open and take proper safety precautions when necessary.

Who's at Risk?

Why would a person need to seek out special security? What factors make one person more likely to be in need of a bodyguard than another? There are various reasons why some people have to be more cautious than others. Their safety is less assured than the average person's. There are a number of reasons why this might be so.

Being trained in self-defense is one way of planning ahead for situations where one's safety is threatened by others.

In the Spotlight

Some people cannot go about their daily lives with any sense of security. There are people that, for whatever reason, are always at higher risk than most. They may be celebrities, like entertainers and sports figures. Celebrities usually enjoy being the center of attention. But they also need to be able to get from place to place without being swamped by fans. And, as in the case of Madonna, they can become easy targets for the criminally insane.

Ransom

Money may also be a motive. A kidnapper who abducts a celebrity stands a good chance of receiving a large ransom in exchange for a rich and widely loved public figure. Business executives may also be at risk for the same reason. Even without superstardom, a wealthy and powerful person in the business world can be an attractive prospect for criminals seeking money and attention.

Activism

Activists are people who work toward making changes in society. For example, animal rights activists hold protests to raise public awareness of cruelty to animals. Antiwar activists look for peaceful solutions to violent conflict. The pro-life movement works toward making abortion an illegal procedure. The list of activist causes goes on and on.

Some activists take their positions to extremes. They may unexpectedly throw blood at fashion designers or models to protest their use of animal fur. Or they may stalk and threaten doctors who perform abortions. Black leaders may be hurt or killed by white supremacist groups, openly gay men and women often risk harassment from antigay activists, and businesspeople can become targets for those who strongly oppose capitalism. Fanatics for their causes have been known to resort to vandalism, sabotage, and even bombs sent through the mail.

A bodyguard stands strong in front of Elijah Muhammad, founder and leader of the Nation of Islam, speaking in Chicago in February 1961. Malcolm X is shown clapping on the left side of the stage.

Government Workers

History has shown us that high-ranking government officials are often put at risk for violence. The most common example is the assassination of a leader, such as the president of the United States. As both politician and celebrity, the president becomes a target for many reasons. Some people believe that killing the representative of a government can help bring about change in the world. They see violence and aggression as the way to bring about better lives for themselves.

Because of the massive power the American government holds, an entire force dedicated to its security is needed. This force is known as the Secret Service. Agents protect the president, the vice president, and their families. Former presidents are protected for ten years after they leave office. The agency also looks after visiting heads of foreign governments and their spouses traveling with them, and official representatives of the United States performing missions abroad.

Victims by Chance

Sometimes ordinary folks with no celebrity or government background find themselves in threatening situations. A person who witnesses a crime might be considered a "high-risk witness." These witnesses may require special protection if there is a chance that they will be threatened, injured, or killed to keep them from testifying in court. Risk is especially high in cases involving gangs or organized crime.

The introduction talked about the stalking of Madonna, a well-known celebrity. But you do not have to be famous to be stalked. Anyone can become a victim of this type of harassment, which may include unwanted phone calls or letters, threatening voice mail or e-mail messages, and being followed persistently. It is estimated that, in the U.S., two percent of all men and 8 percent of all women are stalked at some point in their lives.

The Role of Personal Protection

Like any business, personal protection turns a profit by filling a specialized need in society. Bodyguards

International Bodyguard Association

One extremely important event in the development of modern personal protection was the formation of the International Bodyguard Association (IBA). The organization came about in Paris in 1957. Major Lucien Victor Ott, an important figure in the French military intelligence (Deuxieme Bureau), was told by his superiors to examine the way French military officials were being guarded. He found that the methods being used were not effective. It was now up to Lucien Ott to improve the system.

Ott developed his own method that he named "defense and security." He also assembled a staff of tough bodyguards, veterans of a famous special unit called Les Gorilles, to learn and practice the method. The group trained bodyguard units for kings, presidents, diplomats, politicians, the army, judges, and stars from the media in Europe, Africa, Asia, the Middle East, the Pacific, and Central America. Ott was so devoted to his work that he rarely had time to spend with his wife and two children. The couple divorced, and his wife received custody of their kids.

But while his personal life seemed to suffer, Ott's work continued to flourish. He became a stuntman in Germany for a time and even established a school for stuntmen. In the mid-1970s, he returned to bodyguarding in Brussels, Belgium. There

[*continued from page 15*]
he founded the International Bodyguard Association's Defense and Security Academy. He died of cancer in 1990, leaving behind a legacy of personal protection's most groundbreaking achievements. Today, the IBA has offices all over the world, training and supporting bodyguards who protect everyone from Bill Gates to Bill Clinton.

Being a member of the U.S. Secret Service is perhaps the most prolific bodyguarding post one can achieve. The agent pictured below keeps a vigil over former president Bill Clinton as he addresses an audience on Capitol Hill in 1998.

earn a living making sure their high-risk clients are kept from harm. They help Britney Spears get from her hotel to her concerts without being trampled by adoring fans. They ensure that government officials have the peace of mind to make decisions that affect us all. They help to keep the court system running smoothly by giving witnesses the security they need to do their civic duty and by discouraging would-be criminals. Even if you have never required the skills of a highly trained bodyguard, someday you just might. So isn't it good to know they're around?

Bodyguards Past to Present

On September 6, 1901, a young man succeeded in murdering the president of the United States. His name was Leon Czolgosz, and his motive was anarchy. Czolgosz approached President William McKinley at a reception in a Buffalo, New York, concert hall called the Temple of Music. The assassin walked toward the president with a handkerchief wrapped around his right hand. From under the fabric, he pulled out a .32-caliber handgun and shot McKinley twice.

LESLIE'S WEEKLY

McKINLEY EXTRA

Vol. XCIII—EXTRA NUMBER
Copyright, 1901, by Judge Company, No. 110 Fifth Avenue

New York, September 9, 1901

PRICE 10 CENTS
Entered as second-class matter at the New York Post-Office

Leon Czolgosz, pictured here behind bars, assassinated William McKinley, the twenty-fifth president of the United States, in 1901. This incident led to greater security measures for U.S. presidents.

Czolgosz was an anarchist, a believer in the destruction of all government. He had hoped that killing President McKinley would spread panic among American governing officials and help to advance his cause through mass publicity. The incident forced many people to rethink the issue of government security, and it resulted in a new role for the United States Secret Service. When it was formed in 1865, the agency had been primarily focused on the problem of counterfeit currency. Now they devote all of their resources to protecting the president and other high-ranking officials.

It may be clear to see why the world needs bodyguards. But when and how did this need arise? There was no official starting point for this profession in recorded history. Some say the first bodyguards were samurai warriors of ancient Japan, who were hired by landowners to protect them and their property. The Catholic Church relied on personal protection during the Middle Ages to guard their dignitaries when they traveled. Early protectors of Anglo Saxon tribes' leaders were referred to as their *comitatus* ("companions"), and, like the samurai, they were fiercely loyal to their masters. Some modern bodyguards look to these early examples for inspiration and codes of ethics.

Fighting the Bad Guys

So what do these heroic guardians actually do, besides escorting their clients to parties and stopping would-be intruders in their tracks using brute strength and karate kicks? Probably more than you think. A career as a personal protection specialist is actually as taxing on the mind as it is on the body. It is a path requiring serious commitment to protection at all costs, which demands a quick wit and creative solutions to the problems that are faced in this industry.

Preparation and Prevention

Although many bodyguards are blessed with a strong sense of adventure, they do not want to be hurt while protecting their clients. Nor do they want to pursue attackers on foot or in a car, or use a weapon against anyone. Bodyguards want things to run smoothly. They feel that if personal protection is done properly, nobody else will even know they are there. This means no action sequences, no chase scenes, and no drama if they can be avoided.

And these things are best avoided through planning. A bodyguard needs to anticipate what could

Even someone as physically imposing as basketball star Shaquille O'Neal needs personal protection. Here, his bodyguard, Jerome Crawford, accompanies Shaq during practice in Philadelphia in June 2001.

happen and how it could be prevented. For example, a bodyguard escorts a client to his or her hotel room. What if there is already somebody in the room, waiting to take the client by surprise? A bodyguard must see this as a possible problem and check out the room before the client enters it.

What kind of car is being used to safely get the client from one point to another? Do the doors have strong locks? Are the windows bulletproof? What kind of neighborhoods are on the driving route? Although assignments vary depending on the client, the personal protection specialist is usually responsible for these important safeguards.

Security Technology

Technology plays a key role in a bodyguard's security planning. There are many products on the market designed for personal protection. It is up to the specialist, or the protection agency, to understand these tools. They must know which ones are most effective in different situations, which brands are reputable, and how to use the gear properly.

Bodyguards may sometimes employ surveillance tools, like the miniature hidden camera pictured here, to protect their clients.

Depending on how much the client is willing to pay, a security system can be small or large. It may be as simple as one camera and intercom at the front door of his or her home. Or it might include cameras in every room of the house, "bugs" or small microphones hidden in strategic areas, and sensitive burglar alarms to warn of the slightest movement. These things require some technical know-how to set up, but they also make the bodyguard's job easier, safer, and more effective.

Weapons

Weapons are dangerous things no matter how you look at it. But in the hands of a trained professional, a weapon can save a client's life. Bodyguards try to resist using them until all other options have been tried. But weapons do need to be available in case all else fails, and an agent should be skilled enough with the weapon to use it quickly when the situation calls for it.

Bodyguards who are careless with weapons are a threat to their clients' safety and security, not to mention reputation. It was widely reported that, in February 2000, housing secretary Andrew M. Cuomo's chief bodyguard accidentally left a loaded pistol in a cafeteria. Some of the bodyguard's coworkers said he had left his gun lying around in public places before. This was especially embarrassing to Cuomo, whose political career has been built on issues including gun safety!

The Bodyguarding Career Ladder

Everybody has to start somewhere, and a bodyguard is no exception. They all have to have a first day on the job. Usually a personal protection specialist will start out as a trainee, learning the trade by assisting another bodyguard. This "training through experience" occurs with a bodyguard service or private detective agency. When a trainee is ready, he or she can take on protection assignments on his or her own.

From this point, a bodyguard may advance to case manager and supervise other agents on assignments. The pay generally increases along with the risk and complexity of the work. As a bodyguard gains experience and develops a good reputation, more high-profile clients are drawn in through word of mouth. Assignments with more wealthy and famous clients usually mean more cash and higher prestige. Bodyguards can reach a level of success that allows them to open their own agency or even found a school to pass on their knowledge.

Female Bodyguards

Only 3 percent of the world's bodyguards are female, but the field is open to women who dare to defy the statistics. Female bodyguards are in demand because

Female bodyguards, such as this one in South America, are in demand. Their rarity makes them more appealing to certain clients, such as female clients or those who want to take would-be attackers by surprise.

of their rarity. Some female clients feel more comfortable looking to another woman for personal protection, especially when client and bodyguard are together around the clock. In Japan, it is a trend for businessmen to have female bodyguards who also work as their secretaries.

The BlueBird Women's Bodyguard Team is an all-female group of bodyguards working in Korea. The team was formed in 1997 by the Korea Security Service System (KOSSES), one of the county's leading security agencies. Like an old Hollywood movie studio, the KOSSES carefully controls the image that BlueBird agents show to the public. They are instructed to appear feminine, both to help the clients (often families) easily develop a sense of trust, and to use the element of surprise against would-be attackers. The fact that there are so few women in the profession gives the BlueBirds a special niche to fill.

In the next chapter we will talk about what it really takes to be a success in the personal protection field: skills, training, and, most important, guts.

Brawn, Brains, and Nerves of Steel

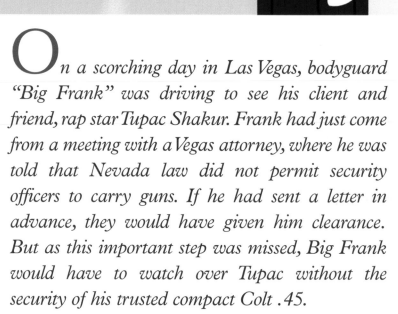

3

On a scorching day in Las Vegas, bodyguard "Big Frank" was driving to see his client and friend, rap star Tupac Shakur. Frank had just come from a meeting with a Vegas attorney, where he was told that Nevada law did not permit security officers to carry guns. If he had sent a letter in advance, they would have given him clearance. But as this important step was missed, Big Frank would have to watch over Tupac without the security of his trusted compact Colt .45.

Tupac was scheduled to perform at a club called 662, a "post-fight" show following a boxing match featuring Mike Tyson. But before the fight, Frank knew he would find Tupac at the Luxor Casino's craps tables because he loved to gamble. Surrounded

An unidentified bodyguard accompanies his boss, rapper Tupac Shakur. Shakur was eventually killed, partly due to a bodyguard's lack of planning.

by beautiful women and draped in gold jewelry, Tupac was losing his game badly. So they moved on to the MGM Grand, hoping for a better payoff.

And pay off it did. At the MGM, Tupac started winning big. Heads turned as his excitement rose, and soon people realized they were in the presence of hip-hop royalty. A small crowd gathered and quickly grew. Frank got a bit nervous. His tension became worse when he realized another grave problem: He did not have his cell phone with him, and he needed to make an important call. So he reluctantly left his client to go in search of a pay phone. When he returned, Tupac was nowhere to be seen.

Frank immediately began to panic. He feared that his client may have been abducted. After a terrifying hour, he finally heard the rapper's voice behind him. The relieved but annoyed bodyguard gave Tupac a stern lecture on the need to rely on personal protection to help prevent dangerous situations. Then he escorted Tupac to the boxing match through a sea of fans shouting for their idol, who continued to snap photographs and ask for his autograph.

After the fight, an acquaintance approached Tupac and whispered something into his ear. Tupac suddenly ran off, his confused protector close behind. Tupac ran to the MGM and immediately began throwing punches at a man Frank did not know. Frank had to pull Tupac away from the scene and try to keep himself between the star, the mystery man, and the police. He wanted to keep his client as far from the chaos as possible.

Frank never found out who the man was or why Tupac had attacked him, but he knew he needed to keep a close eye on the troubled star for the rest of the night. They decided to make their way to the club where Tupac would be performing. Tupac was in the passenger seat of a friend's car, while Frank followed closely behind. Both cars stopped at a red light, and Big Frank watched as a gun poked out of a nearby white Cadillac to fire at his client. Minutes later, Tupac Shakur was dead.

Sharp as a Tack

The story of Big Frank and Tupac shows how complicated bodyguarding can be. Many people see a bodyguard as a mass of muscle, without a mind or heart. But a personal protection specialist must have all three in large amounts. Of course, the muscle is important. Agencies hiring bodyguards look for those in excellent physical condition, and even experienced agents know that taking good care of their bodies helps them take good care of their clients. You cannot guard another body without guarding your own first.

Most bodyguards would probably agree that mental clarity is what their job most requires. For example, Big Frank felt unsure about that night in Las Vegas from the very beginning because he had failed to think ahead and clear his weapon with the state of Nevada. And why did he not have his cell phone when he needed it? Planning and attention to detail are skills, and a personal protection specialist must develop them before taking on assignments. He or she must spend a great deal of time considering situations that could arise throughout the upcoming workday, week, month, or year. There must be plans for dealing with problems and alternate plans in case the first set of plans falls through. One can never be too thorough when lives are at stake.

An assassination attempt on President Ronald Reagan in 1981 left injured bystanders. Secret Service agents must make quick decisions to handle such situations properly.

A bodyguard's reflex time must be quick because when dangerous situations arise, things happen fast and people lose control. The agent must be able to think on his or her feet and make decisions. Difficult decisions must be made in a heartbeat. Madonna's bodyguard, Basil Stephens, did not have time to ponder questions of life and death when he shot at the intruder on his client's estate. He made an immediate decision, and if the stalker died from the gunshot, Stephens would have to live with his decision for the rest of his life. Many people would not be able to make a logical choice in such intense situations. That's true brain power.

Bodyguards Are "People People"

You may not think of personal protection as a business that relies upon "people skills." But protecting others is at the heart of being a bodyguard. This means caring about people, being attentive to their needs, and form-ing intimate relationships based on trust. A client's bodyguard is often also a good friend. In some cases, such as actress Roseanne Arnold with Ben Thomas, Princess Stephanie of Monaco with Daniel Ducruet, and tennis star Venus Williams with David Tomassoni, the agent becomes even more than a friend. All of these well-known clients formed romantic relationships with their bodyguards!

It makes sense that close, personal bonds would develop between clients and protectors. They spend a great deal of time together, sharing experiences, and clients depend upon bodyguards to keep them safe. The client can feel like a child in some ways, looking to a parent for safety and security. They need a shield between themselves and the raging sea of fans and media.

If the chemistry is not right between agent and client, the results can be disastrous. Actor Mark Wahlberg, formerly rapper Marky Mark, was sued by his former bodyguard for attacking him in a public place. The agent, Leonard Taylor, claimed that Wahlberg not only beat him with his fists but bit his arm as well. A relationship has to go pretty sour to result in teeth-marks and tetanus shots!

Client-bodyguard romances are not just fairy tales of the silver screen: both actress Roseanne Arnold *(left)* and Princess Stephanie became involved with their respective protectors!

Training and Experience

Education for a bodyguard position is easily found. There are countless schools that specialize in training and job placement for aspiring agents. The Executive Protection Institute offers courses such as So You Want to Be a Personal Protection Specialist (PPS), Urban Terrorism, and Managing Security Systems. The Bodyguard School and Training Program at the Center for Advanced Security Studies offers bodyguard training with worldwide placement, focusing on jobs available in South America. And the International Bodyguard Association offers respected training programs in both basic protection and specialized areas such as Aviation Escort and VIP Hotel Security.

It is up to an agency to decide what type of education their agents need to have. Some require only a high school diploma, while others may consider only college graduates or those with specialized training. Experience can make a difference as well. Many bodyguards come from other fields, such as law enforcement or the military. Those with proven track records, such as police officers or military officials, may not be expected to seek more training.

All bodyguards, whether through training or experience, need to be mature and disciplined. Their driving skills must be top-notch. They should also be experts in unarmed self-defense techniques, such as karate and jujitsu. And they need to have a thorough understanding of security technology and prevention measures.

License to Defend

This corporate logo for the Executive Protection Institute, a bodyguard school, exemplifies the qualities of bravery and dedication required of bodyguards.

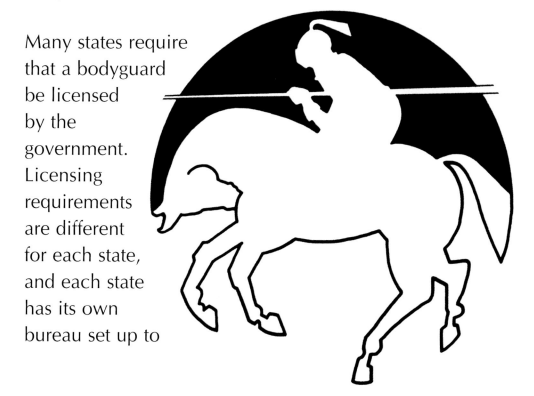

Many states require that a bodyguard be licensed by the government. Licensing requirements are different for each state, and each state has its own bureau set up to enforce its particular laws. To receive a license, a bodyguard may need to be within the state's age limits and reach a certain level of education and experience. The agent may also have to complete training through certified organizations (schools that are approved by the state). And in some bureaus a personal protection specialist must be approved for a private investigator's license.

Money and Competition

So how much dough do these loyal defenders actually earn for their efforts? Pay scales vary tremendously, depending upon the wealth of the client, the experience and reputation of the agent, and the nature of the assignment. But a general estimate is between $100 and $500 per day.

Competition in the field can become intense because of the large number of military and police officers who enter the profession. Those applicants have a definite edge over people from other backgrounds. Training with a reputable school is also a huge plus for most agencies.

Toward a
Safer
Future

4

When Diana, Princess of Wales, was tragically killed in a 1997 car crash, many called it "the crash heard around the world." She was riding with her boyfriend, Dodi Al Fayed, in the backseat of a Mercedes. The car was being pursued by paparazzi (newspaper and magazine photographers) on motorcycles, who hoped to catch a candid photo of the princess with Dodi. The Mercedes sped into an underpass near France's Eiffel Tower on the River Seine and crashed into a pillar. Dodi was killed instantly, while Diana passed away after two hours of surgery on her heart.

Diana and Dodi's chauffeur that night, Henri Paul, who was also killed, had shown poor

Trevor Rees-Jones, the only survivor of the car crash that killed Diana, Princess of Wales, her boyfriend, Dodi Al Fayed, and their chauffeur, Henri Paul, looks visibly shaken after being interviewed by authorities about the accident.

judgment by drinking before driving. His blood alcohol content was later found to have been more than three times the legal limit! Paul was also driving too quickly, according to Trevor Rees-Jones, Dodi's bodyguard and the only survivor of the crash. The driver's actions seemed especially shocking because of his important position as assistant chief of security for the Paris Ritz Hotel.

Rees-Jones suffered severe head and facial injuries in the accident, and he endured a coma and major surgery. But perhaps even worse, he awoke to find himself one of the key figures in what may go down as the worst personal protection mishap of all time. The shaken bodyguard later told the British newspaper the Daily Telegraph, *"If I could have died and those three survived, I would have done it. If I could have done something . . . I go mad thinking about if onlys." He has openly discussed his feelings of guilt and shame about the accident that took the life of a beloved princess and her dear friend.*

Learning from the Past

So what happened? Clearly the driver was an irresponsible member of the security team. But some people believe that bodyguard Rees-Jones was not properly taking care of his client. Should he have been more aware of the driver's condition? Should he have been more forceful and demanded that Paul pull over when he began speeding? Might he have planned a better driving route for the group, so as to avoid the underpass where they crashed as well as the paparazzi that were following them? Rees-Jones has asked himself these questions. And although he does feel a heavy sense of survivor's guilt, he believes that the person truly responsible was Dodi Al Fayed, for instructing the chauffeur to drive at a high speed.

Some disagree with Rees-Jones's conclusion. Dr. Richard W. Kobetz, director of the Executive Protection Institute (EPI), sees the incident as an example of people trying to save money by hiring unqualified personal protection specialists. Trevor Rees-Jones was an army paratrooper before going to work as "Dodi's shadow." Henri Paul was a paratrooper captain in the French air

Henri Paul *(left)* confers with Diana and Dodi Al Fayed at the Ritz Hotel in Paris, with Trevor Rees-Jones in the background, shortly before the tragic accident.

force. Kobetz states on the EPI's official Web site (http://www.personalprotection.com), "Standing alone, [their military experiences were] high qualifications indeed, which tends to reinforce the notion that anyone can protect anyone else. But really, can anyone protect anyone else? On what type of a measurement scale of protection performance? Would not one acknowledge there might be more than a slight difference between someone hired as a 'bodyguard' from a day labor office, and a fully trained, certified and qualified executive/personal protection specialist?"

The Importance of Specialized Training

Kobetz's point was that although both men had military experience, they were not well trained in the special problems faced by celebrity clients. In his book, *The Bodyguard's Story: Diana, the Crash, and the Sole Survivor*, Rees-Jones claims to have taken only two civilian close-protection courses to learn the basics. Dodi's staff found the bodyguard by placing an advertisement in a military employment newspaper, not through a personal protection agency or school. And although Dodi was wealthy, he did not begin to attract media attention until he began seeing Diana. The sudden change in his working environment may have caught Rees-Jones off guard.

The bodyguard also wrote about his difficulty in adjusting to differences between military work and personal protection. In the military, one is given definite orders and a regular schedule. Personal protection requires more diplomacy, decision making, and flexibility. It also requires the strength to say no to a client who makes risky demands. Rees-Jones explained that Dodi often pushed him to drive at high speeds. And while he would usually ignore his boss's prodding, he did occasionally drive faster to keep the peace with Dodi.

Future Technology

Security technology is always growing, and personal protection specialists must stay up-to-date on the latest gadgets. Bulletproof vests keep getting stronger and more lightweight. Armored cars are available with useful and exciting features, like smoke screens, sirens, megaphones, devices to track other vehicles, and tough shielding from many powerful weapons. Wristwatch cameras can be used to keep tabs on suspicious characters. High-tech aerosol sprays can be used to detect the presence of explosives. Night vision goggles allow agents to keep tabs on intruders approaching in the dead of night, and portable metal detectors can help detect the presence of hidden guns or explosives.

New security gadgets, like these night vision goggles, are a must for many personal protection professionals.

An agent may not use every high-tech gadget that hits the market or set up a complex security system for every client. The process is a bit more complicated than that. Bodyguards do need to be aware of the technology available, as well as how it is used. But more important, they need to determine the best use of equipment for each particular assignment. Some clients may be best served by certain types of gear, while others might require a completely different setup. It all depends upon the client's lifestyle and the nature of the assignment.

A Different World

On September 11, 2001, ideas about security and protection changed all over the world. That was the day that terrorists crashed airplanes full of passengers into New York City's tallest buildings, as well as the Pentagon near Washington, D.C., and a field in Pennsylvania. Thousands were killed, and many more injured and traumatized. Parents, siblings, children, spouses, and best friends were lost forever.

People are still asking how this could have happened. Suddenly we do not feel as safe as we used to. We wonder if the basic sense of security we once enjoyed is gone forever. Such a violent and terrifying event has affected many areas of the business world, and the personal protection industry is no exception. Bodyguards must face new questions, which may not yet have answers. In protecting clients, is there any possible way to prepare for terrorist attacks of such scale? What kinds of special precautions need to be taken during times of war?

Biological Attacks

One threat that some people feel unprepared for is an attack using chemical and biological weapons (CBW), also referred to as bioterrorism. This type of attack involves the use of substances that are dangerous to living things. These substances can cause injury or death, and may be spread through water, air, and even the mail.

The biological weapon people seem to be talking about most since September 11 is anthrax. Anthrax is a

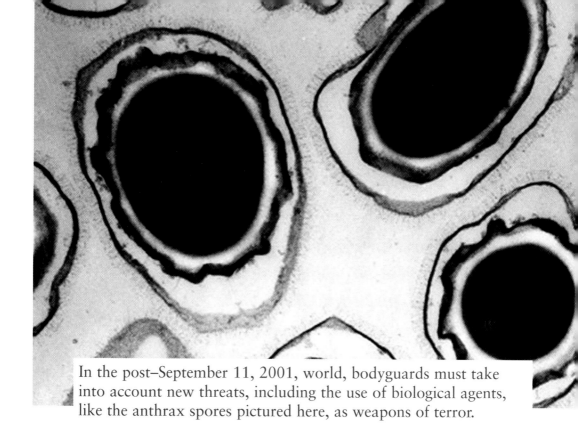

In the post–September 11, 2001, world, bodyguards must take into account new threats, including the use of biological agents, like the anthrax spores pictured here, as weapons of terror.

disease that is spread in the form of a powder that releases deadly spores into the atmosphere. Security agents today, especially those protecting government officials, test their clients' mail and surroundings for the deadly poison. While anthrax is usually treatable, it can cause great suffering and, in some cases, death.

Personal protection specialists must do all they can to protect their clients from anthrax and other CBWs if the clients are at risk. Special gear, such as gas masks or machinery to test air quality, may be needed.

Agencies and schools are also adding courses to their curricula that teach bodyguards how to handle these new threats to personal security.

Cutting-Edge Education

Bodyguards, as well as bodyguards-in-training, have much more to educate themselves about besides CBWs. They must learn the history of terrorism in order to understand the many violent methods fanatical groups have used in the past. And they need to be on the cutting edge of newly developing terror threats as well. The Executive Protection Institute has been teaching about these issues since 1978. One of their current courses, called Urban Terrorism, provides the most up-to-date information on topics such as executive protection on airplanes, tactics for dealing with "air rage" (violent airplane passengers), the motivations for terrorism, panic control, and protection of possible terrorist targets, just to name a few.

The Enemies Within

Another special problem that could surface more often in the coming years is that of dangerous people impersonating bodyguards. Terrorists know that people trust security agents. They might try to say they are on a security staff to protect a client in order to gain access to restricted areas or carry weapons without looking suspicious. They can also create false identification cards to back up their lies. Some counterfeit International Bodyguard Association cards have been found in the possession of criminals, and the IBA issued warnings about the phony IDs. Agencies that hire bodyguards or trainees now perform stricter background checks on applicants than ever before.

But even the act of guarding against this problem has its own complications. On December 25, 2001, a bodyguard assigned to protect President George W. Bush tried to board an American Airlines flight. The Secret Service agent, who was of Arabic descent, was asked by the pilot to leave the plane because he was suspected of terrorism. According to the agent, he

Security concerns after the terrorist attacks on the United States in September 2001 have seemingly made everyone more cautious. President George W. Bush is pictured talking on the phone to New York City Mayor Rudy Giuliani.

was singled out because of racial bias. But the airline claims that the bodyguard was behaving suspiciously, carried a weapon, and failed to fill out security forms properly.

Growing Concerns, Growing Need

In the wake of September 11, personal protection specialists may find themselves more in demand than ever. The president and vice president of the United States require greater protection since the attacks. Many celebrities, like superstar vocalist Barbra Streisand, hired additional bodyguards after the tragedies. Government officials and business executives are taking security precautions they may not have in the past. While this growing awareness can hardly be called a silver lining to terrorism's dark cloud, it does mean more opportunities for those in the personal protection field. People today are more willing to spend money to protect themselves and those around them.

As the world changes, so does the role of the bodyguard. Security may be the top concern of the United States as we continue to fight a war against uncertain enemies. In many ways, personal protection is at the center of what our government calls a world changed forever. But what will not change is the dedication and courage of bodyguards, our modern-day samurai warriors. And hopefully, there will always be a fierce and loyal group of people to protect all that we value.

Glossary

activist A person who works toward making changes in society.

air rage The act of becoming violent while aboard a plane in transit.

anarchist A believer in the destruction of all government.

bias A prejudiced outlook.

bioterrorism The use of dangerous substances, such as anthrax spores, to promote terror.

case manager A personal protection agent who supervises other agents on assignments.

counterfeit Made in imitation of something; false.

dignitary A person who is in a position of honor or prestige; a person who holds a special rank.

diplomacy A special skill involving the ability to negotiate without hostility.

high-risk witness Someone who runs the risk of being threatened, injured, or killed because he or she witnessed a certain crime.

mishap An unfortunate event; an accident; bad luck.

paparazzi Aggressive and often intrusive newspaper and magazine photographers who seek to photograph celebrities.

samurai warriors Hired protectors of land owners and their property in ancient Japan.

security technology Equipment used to aid in personal protection.

stalking Harassment that may include unwanted phone calls or letters, threatening voice mail or e-mail messages, and persistent following.

United States Secret Service The security agency dedicated to protecting the United States president and other government officials.

For More Information

Center for Advanced Security Studies
P.O. Box 1482
Naples, FL 34106-1482
e-mail: bodyguardschool@aol.com
Web site: http://www.bodyguardschool.com

Executive Protection Institute (EPI)
P.O. Box 802
Berryville, VA 22611
(540) 554-2540
Web site: http://www.personalprotection.com

International Association of Personal
    Protection Agents
P.O. Box 266
Arlington Heights, IL 60006-0266

(847) 870-8007
Web site: http://www.iappa.org

International Bodyguard Association North America
P.O. Box 675344
Rancho Santa Fe, CA 92067-5344
(858) 756-6806
Web site: http://www.ibabodyguards.com

In Canada

International Bodyguard Association Canada
8003 Argyll Road
Edmonton, AB T6C 4A9
(780) 461-5700
Web site: http://www.ibabodyguards.com

Web Sites

Due to the changing nature of Internet links, the Rosen Publishing Group, Inc., has developed an online list of Web sites related to the subject of this book. This site is updated regularly. Please use this link to access the list:

http://www.rosenlinks.com/ec/body/

For Further Reading

Arnold, Terrell, and Moorhead Kennedy. *Think About Terrorism: The New Warfare.* New York: Walker and Co. Library, 1991.

Echaore-McDavid, Susan. *Career Opportunities in Law Enforcement, Security, and Protective Services.* New York: Facts on File, Inc., 2000.

Goodnough, David. *Stalking: A Hot Issue.* Berkeley Heights, NJ: Enslow Publishing, 2000.

Keny, Zachary. *William McKinley.* Chicago: Children's Press, 1988.

Kilgore, Kristie. *Eyes Wide Open: Bodyguard Strategies for Self-Protection.* New Castle, CO: Clinetop Press, 2001.

Landau, Elaine. *Big Brother Is Watching: Secret Police and Intelligence Services.* New York: Walker and Co. Library, 1992.

Oleksy, Walter G. *Princess Diana.* San Diego, CA: Lucent Books, 2000.

Turnbull, Stephen R. *The Samurai Sourcebook.* London: Cassell, 1998.

Bibliography

ABC News. "The Sole Survivor: A Chat with Bodyguard Trevor Rees-Jones." March 21, 2000. Retrieved March 2002 (http://abcnews.go.com/sections/world/dailynews/chat_reesjones0321.html).

Anderson, Kevin. BBC News. "Bush Bodyguard Alleges Racial Bias." January 2, 2002. Retrieved March 2002 (http://news.bbc.co.uk/hi/english/world/americas/newsid_1741000/1741580.stm).

Associated Press. "A Bodyguard's Tale Awaits." September 5, 1997. Retrieved March 2002 (http://www.canoe.ca/PrincessDiana/sep5_bodyguard.html).

Echaore-McDavid, Susan. *Career Opportunities in Law Enforcement, Security, and Protective Services.* New York: Facts on File, Inc., 2000.

Entertainment Tonight Online. "Star Bodyguard Romances." August 16, 2000. Retrieved March 2002 (http://www.etonline.com/celebrity/a5694.htm).

HoustonChronicle.com. "The Life and Death of a Princess." Retrieved March 2002 (http://www.chron.com/content/chronicle/special/princess/index.html).

Rees-Jones, Trevor, and Moira Johnston. *The Bodyguard's Story: Diana, the Crash, and the Sole Survivor.* New York: Warner Books, Inc., 2000.

Time.com. "Partial Recall: Survivor Trevor Rees-Jones Begins to Remember the Accident That Claimed the Life of Princess Diana." March 16, 1998. Retrieved March 2002 (http://www.time.com/time/daily/special/diana/readingroom/sept9798/8.html).

Index

About the Author

John Giacobello is a freelance writer living in New York City.

Photo Credits

Cover © FPG/Getty Images; p. 6 © Mitchell Gerber/ Corbis; p. 9 © Paul A. Souders/Corbis; pp. 12, 16, 21, 23, 26, 29, 35, 40, 43, 49, 52 © AP/Wide World Photos; p. 18 © The Library of Congress, Prints and Photographs Division; p. 33 © Corbis; p. 37 courtesy of the Executive Protection Institute; p. 46 © Jeffrey L. Rotman/Corbis.

Design

Les Kanturek

Layout

Tahara Hasan